SELF-RESCUE: Battling and Beating PTSD

2nd Edition

Brett Kraykovic

ISBN: 9798370583742

Front cover image by Brett Kraykovic

Book design by Brett Kraykovic

Disclaimer

This book is written as if I was talking to another soldier, or a friend going through the same shit. I use terrible language, I am blunt and to the point. This book also WILL NOT CURE YOU! It will help you manage the symptoms of PTSD, but you will not magically be cured of all your ailments. It can make you feel like you are cured, but you are not. You will still have break through PTSD symptoms from time to time and this book will help you there are well.

This book is not definitive medical advice; I am not a Doctor, Therapist, or anything of the sort. This book represents what I have done to deal with C-PTSD/PTSD, Anxiety, Panic Attacks and Depression for 20 years. It works like a charm for me, but some of it, or hell, all of it may not work for you.

The methods here do work, but I must suggest not stopping any current treatment or medications you are currently using. The mental health system may be completely fucked up, but it does work for some. So stay the course if you were lucky enough to not get totally screwed by the system.

Each chapter will have space afterwards where there will be some questions, and space to write your own thoughts. If you bought this as an E-Book, get the paperback, easier to refer to and to complete the extra sections.

Finally, of course if you are thinking of hurting yourself or others, GET HELP! Call the Suicide/Crisis hotline: 988. Reach out to a buddy, family or you can probably find me online somewhere, you can talk to me. But for God's sake, talk to SOMEONE!

For Karen: Thank you

Contents

Prologue

I was a soldier for 20 years. I dedicated my life to my country. After all I sacrificed, suffered and did for the good ol' US of A, imagine my surprise when I got out with issues accrued through the years, and that the Government did not and could not help me.

My issues really started around 2002. PTSD, TBI, and a destroyed back, I got 800 milligram Motrin on a regular basis, seems to have been their cure for everything. Thinking back I remember wondering what was wrong with me. I wasn't functioning mentally as I had used to. Nightmares, migraines, anxiety and panic attacks, were all new to me, leaving me confused and afraid. I started doing what most soldiers do, I self-medicated with alcohol. I did not let my fellow soldiers know what was going on, another thing that most soldiers do, hide it. I tried telling myself;

"Just suck it up; it's all just in your head."

"It's due to the divorce, nothing else."

"Push through, embrace the suck, quit being a pussy!"

It all caught up to me one day, I was extremely depressed and despondent. I could no longer do my job, or function around others, I couldn't even take care of myself. I was getting into trouble with my command as well. I would go out to the local bars just to drink, get into fights and find women. I was at total rock bottom.

I had decided that since my career in the Army was pretty much over, I was just gonna end it. In my head, if I couldn't hop and pop, sneak and peek, or jump anymore, I had no reason to go on. I spent years in training getting into the Special Ops community, and now it was over.

I drank another bottle of Smirnoff, pulled out my vintage K-Bar (not as sharp as I would have wanted) and proceeded to peel the median artery out of my left arm. I watched the blood pump out of my arm as I felt as if I was being lowered into a warm bath. Then it all faded to black.

I woke up in the hospital, or came too more like it. I was pissed off! I was alive and in my mind I failed at suicide as well as everything else! But, deep down, as I sobered up from the gallons of IV fluid pumping into me, I was relieved. Somehow I was glad to be alive. This wasn't my first brush with death, or my last, but this one deeply affected me somehow.

The Army in their infinite wisdom decided that regardless of PTSD, TBI and back injuries, they gave me an honorable discharge due to a "Personality Disorder". That kept them from having to give me a medical rating, and they could wash their hands of me.

I headed home, vodka in hand. I wandered for almost a year, job to crappy job, lost in mind, body and soul. Turns out that the Army giving me a "personality disorder" discharge worked to my benefit in the end. I found a contractor for the Dept. of Justice (name withheld at their request) that was hiring ex-soldiers just like me!

I started working for said contractor, in Mexico/South America in general. We were doing hostage recovery and drug interdiction. I was a mess! It was one big drunken party really, doing what I loved without the threat of command busting my rank again, or consequences really; we were just mercenaries for the US, doing what we were told as we saw fit.

Needless to say all of this did nothing for my mental health. It covered up my issues, I drown them out with Vodka, but I could be unstable and still be handsomely rewarded for it.

I did this for around 6 months, until I was at the bottom again, but I had some money, so I had hoped I could get some help finally. I headed home once again. I kept up with the self-medicating for another 13 years, another marriage, and two more kids, until years later I met someone who seemed to actually care about what I was going through.

Throughout the years I had a little journal that I wrote down things that would help me during times of sobriety. After I met my new wife, I was forced (in a good way) to start making use of the things I had been learning. She pushed me to fight the VA to get benefits, and to start taking care of myself instead of others all the time. After 3 years I was able to get VA benefits, they finally admitted to the PTSD, the TBI and even my back. In hopes of getting help with my mental health, my wife sent me off to rehab at the VA two weeks after our wedding. But we were disappointed, yet not surprised to find the mental health system at the VA is lacking unless I wanted to transition to a woman.

So we started working on the "Self-Rescue" plan. She is my "care taker" per say, she has helped me at my lowest times, and still does. But the most important thing is how she supports me in my journey to "Fuck-it".

So here we are now, I got my system working, and I am still married! We are doing better than ever. Of course there are speed bumps and setbacks along the path, but I don't have to rely on anyone for help anymore. I've figured out how to "Self-Rescue".

Due to the type of Wife I have, she was the one who suggested I write it all down to help others. She doesn't approve of the language, but she knows I had to do it my way. So, there you have it, a short version of my history and how I got to where I am today.

1: "Self-Rescue" Mindset

Now on to the meat of things. The "Self-Rescue" mind set, or as I lovingly call it; the "Fuck-it" mindset. It is actually a pretty simple theory. There are some steps you need to take, it definitely doesn't happen overnight and it is something you have to consciously work on every-fucking-day. Nothing comes easy as a lot of you know, especially if it's totally worth it in the end.

I spent 20 years in the Army as I've said before, I went for every school I could, the harder the better. Special Forces, Ranger, Sapper. None were easy, but all were worth it. Getting the tabs were some of the best days of my life. Then I suddenly found myself out of the Special Operations community, the Military completely. I was screwed up, unable to function mentally. So what did I do? I tried to kill myself because I thought my life was over without all I had worked my ass off for. I tried to take the easy way out after all I had gone through. My mindset was way off. I was able to finish some of the toughest training in the Army, but I could not handle not having control of my brain. Compared to the training I've been through, taking myself back was a walk in the park. I just needed a map, which I did not have at the time.

So I started looking at myself differently. Yes I was different. I wasn't the quiet professional, self-assured and cocky as hell like I used to be. I was a shell of who I was and couldn't believe I had let myself somehow get to that point. But I realized something pretty early on that helped a lot, it wasn't my fault. It wasn't because I was weak, or off my game. It was what it was and I couldn't just rub some dirt on it and drive on. I had to find my way on my own and make myself as whole as I could for the sake of my kids, (wives/partners as well if you've had less than three). I was setting an example for my children, who they needed to look up to. They were seeing me every night drunk and moping in my recliner and that was not the example I wanted to set.

After years of pain, frustration, being failed by the system and lots of self-doubt I finally found my path. Found my "Map" you could say. I started writing things down, and this little book is the result. I hope you find this useful, if I can help one person other than myself though the hell of PTSD then it's all been worth it.

I apologize for the rambling, but it's my book, so go do something else if you can't take a little rambling here and there.

Step-one: The Beginning

The first and most important step is simple in theory, but can take some serious working through. They say the first step is the hardest, for some this will be. You <u>need</u> to accept your own mortality. The best way I heard it put is by the great Tyler Durden, (Fight Club). "First, You've Gotta Know – Not Fear, Know – That Someday, You're Gonna Die."

Death is in itself a scary thing for most. It's the fear of pain and the unknown. Some of us have watched others pass away; some have seen others killed or die in terrible ways. Deep down no one really wants to die. We want to live, travel and spend time with our loved ones. But that primal fear of death always sits in the back of everyone's mind.

If you drill down to the root of all fears, it usually ends in a fear of pain which can be drilled down to a fear of death. Take panic attacks for example; you feel like you are dying, chest hurts, you feel and your mind is telling you that you are having a heart attack. Then your adrenaline kicks in making everything worse! Damn Fight or Flight, (this will be covered in another section) it ramps all the terrible feelings up and lets your mind run riot. This makes it worse and then your mind continues fucking with you until it feels like it has done its job and screwed you up mentally and physically, then disappears. Then to make things even more screwed up, you start to develop anxiety about having another panic attack. Then you have entered the eternal circle of shit, having anxiety about a panic attack can cause a panic attack, lovely how that works right? All of it boiling down to the feeling that the attack is going to kill you.

Personally until I realized the reality of how a panic attack truly affects me, I probably went to the emergency room thinking I was dying over 30+ times in the last 20 years. The ER doctors could see me coming a mile away, give me an EKG, reassure me my heart is fine and shoot me up with some Benzo and send me home until next time.

So, in accepting that life is short, and that you will be in the dirt at some point in the not too distant future. You can say to yourself;

"This hasn't killed me the last 100 times it's happened."

Or,

"This hasn't killed me yet, let it try."

Getting this simple mindset can help with a whole array of issues, Depression, PTSD, Anxiety, and Panic Attacks. Just go with the feelings, embrace them, and make them your bitch. Know in your head and heart that it's not going to kill you, and if it does, well shit happens. Pick a fight with the feelings, egg them on. When you feel an attack start, reach out for it and grab on, own it. In your mind, dare it to make you feel like you are dying, give it permission to do its worst. Taking away its power is a huge stride towards owning your mortality. This takes trial and error, trips to the ER, and days of lying in bed. One word of caution though; if it does feel different, not your usual attacks, go to the ER just for safety's sake. Don't be dumb and fight through a real heart attack.

Once you've accepted your own mortality, it's time to move to the next step; Setting routines.

Step-two: Routines

Routines are an important life addition for someone dealing with the PTSD symptoms mentioned in this book, it is a vital and important mindset to have. Setting and keeping routines will not only help with self-care, but give you your control back. If you are anything like I was at my worst, I didn't shower regularly, I didn't brush my teeth, I just didn't take care of myself in general. Neglecting self-care can and will cause other health issues in the future, that is why it is imperative to get your routines set up. Here is an example of the routine that I currently use;

8am wake up, pee, start coffee then have a smoke while coffee brews, take a shit, drink first cup of coffee, smoke, drink second cup, smoke, shower, shave, brush teeth. All this done before 10am on a perfect day. To avoid staring at the walls and letting your mind race while you drink your coffee, or tea or whatever read a book. I've amassed quite the library of books for just this purpose.

I apologize for the potty words, but saying shit is easier than writing defecating. Plus, if you are offended already, this most likely isn't the book for you, so fuck off and go color something in your safe space.

It's a simple routine that gets me going for the day, and has an extra added benefit. While I am concentrating on my routine, I forget the nightmares I just woke up from, a huge plus on having a good day. Of course your routine will be different, but adding the important daily activities at the beginning of your day, it gives you a morale boost first thing in the morning.

Now I had my back destroyed while in the Army, I just got it fixed, (3 years of begging the VA) so soon I will add exercise into my routine. I'll get those good ol' endorphins, nature's mood enhancer.

Adding a good thing to your routine is fine, what you do not want to do is subtract from your routine unless it is causing you issues. As simple as a routine is, fucking it up will 100% ruin your whole god damn day. It may take a bit to find the right combination, but remember, include good hygiene and something positive. Don't stare at your phone in the morning, stay off social media, and stay away from the news. That shit is not positive; it's negativity staring right back at you.

I cannot stress enough how important it is to keep your routine. Sometimes life will happen and you won't be home to enact your planned routine. So, you must then pre-plan ahead for this. I had to go to Hawaii for my Step-Daughters wedding, obviously not home, but also not a terrible place to have to go—so I pre-planned a routine, made sure I knew where I could get coffee every morning, let my wife know how much time I needed in the morning to compose myself. She does hate how long it takes me to get myself together by the way, but it is what it is. It all worked out well while I was there, the ocean didn't hurt either, helped with my relaxation. But I did fall off the wagon while there, but that's another story. Anyway...

I've included some space so you can write in your own routines, use it, dog ear the pages so you can refer to it or you'll forget it like I do.

MY DAILY ROUTINE

____

____

____

____

____

____

____

____

____

____

____

____

____

____

____

____

So at this point, you are working on no longer being afraid of death, have a good routine going and feeling pretty good a few hours after waking up, so what's next? **The true Fuck-it stage**.

The Fuck-it stage is pretty much how it sounds. It's a way at looking at life through new eyes, or your younger eyes. How I got to the Fuck-it stage was I thought back to a time when I was a bad-ass in the Army, how did I look at life then? Did little shit bother me? Hell no. That's Fuck-it. It may be different for you, but reach back to when you felt invincible, or unfazed by things. When you could drink until 4am and run PT at 4:30am. Finding your past self before you were fucked up in the head is important. Finding that time in your life when you were totally in control of how you felt.

PTSD, Anxiety, and Panic Attacks have a trigger 99% of the time. It is identifying your triggers and looking at them as little fucking annoyances instead of triggers. Little things, like someone walking to close behind me in Wal-Mart used to set me off. Now since Fuck-it came along, I turn around and kindly ask them to back the fuck up, instead of getting anxiety over it. This gives me control in that situation; I'm controlling my own feelings and surroundings.

Sometimes you cannot control your surroundings, and that's ok, just walk away. Maybe a family member on your cousins-uncles-roommates side is annoying the hell out of you, setting off triggers. Walk away, fuck what anyone else thinks. This is about YOU and your mental health, not pleasing anyone else. It does make it tougher when you are married; diplomacy is needed during the use of "Fuck-it". You can't just tell your wife that some plans in the future will be a trigger; you have to pre-plan your responses to these situations and give yourself an escape plan. This can also apply to work situations, having to take an early lunch, or a walk around the block to get away is ok. Use simple escapes so you are not smothered by everyone asking if you are "Ok", if you are like me that is just as annoying as any other trigger.

Using a bit of diplomacy can also help with not adding extra stress in your life, like having to find a new job, or a new wife, house, dog...

I went and had a tattoo done to help me remember my target mindset. It is a skull and crossbones with "mne pohui" written under it. Roughly translated it means "I don't give a fuck" in Russian. I slap it when something is bothering me, reminding myself, that in fact, I don't give a fuck.

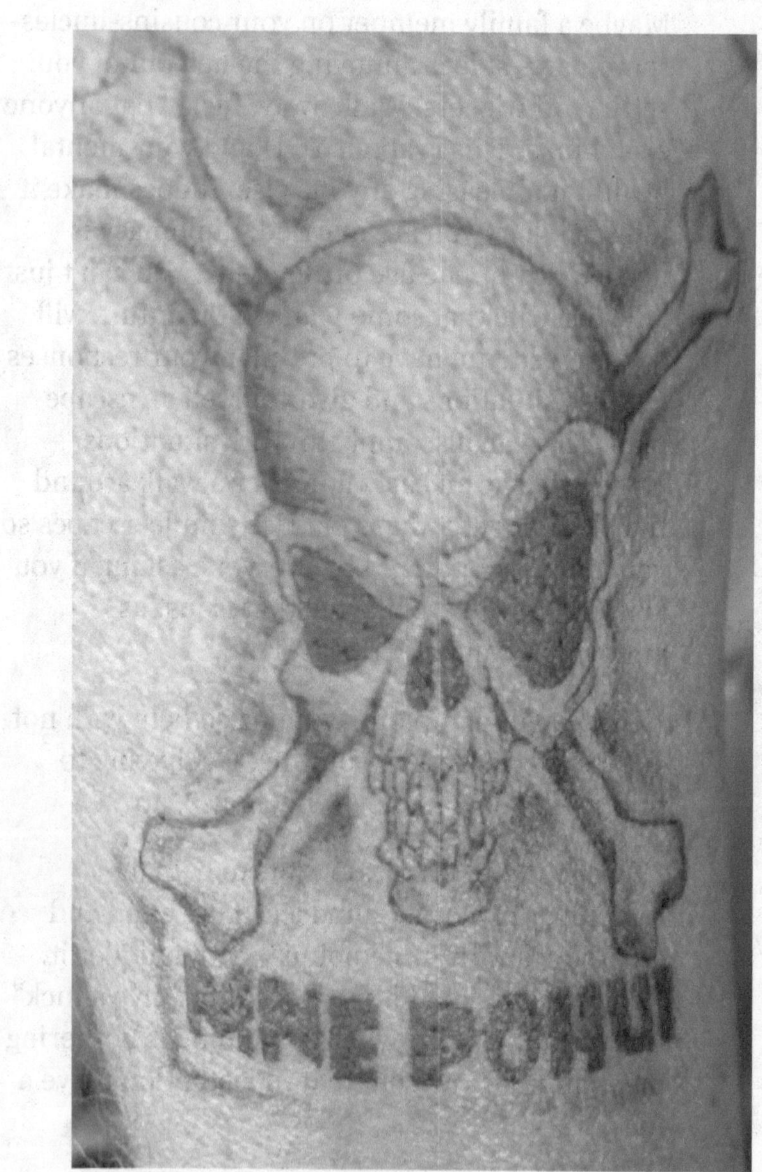

MNE POHUI

Fuck-it can be used in any situation. Hear a bump in the night that sets your hyper vigilance off? I now hope it is some dumb bastard breaking into my house so he can help me test my new 124gr hollow point reloads. Someone wants to argue? Walk away. Fuck-it, it is not worth it. Don't sweat the little things, put them below you. They do not matter and cannot and will not affect you if you take control. Soon you will be viewing the annoyances that used to set you off as nothing to be concerned about. Save your anxiety for some real stressors, like a divorce, or a death in the family.

You have to remind yourself after your routine that you are in control of your own well-being. Remember that YOU and YOU alone are in control of how you feel. With practice you will achieve this mindset. It is not easy, takes actually doing it. But do it, like I said; only YOU can control how you feel and react to things.

As I have said "Fuck-it" doesn't happen overnight, nothing of value ever does. It takes practice to look at something that is really stressing you out and make a conscious choice to not look at it as you used to. At first your mind will be the one telling you flat out that you should be, and need to be stressed. It's changing this reaction that will be the key to it all. When something hits you, analyze it. Take it apart in your mind, this will not only help with looking at things different, but distract from the stress of it. Ask yourself:

"Is this really that bad?"

"Why does that bother me so badly?"

"Why is this little horseshit bugging me? Why am I letting it?"

Question everything that triggers you, once you start mastering it, if you are confident enough, start putting yourself into situations just so you CAN question it. If going to Walmart stresses you out, make a trip to just walk around and deal with it. This goes for anything that stresses you out.

Talking to creditors or making calls at all can set off anger and stress in some people. So how do we handle it? We put it off, usually until it's too late and we get even more stress due to getting sued. Take care of issues as they happen, be proactive, not reactive when it come to stressors and triggers. This will give you your control back.

Fight or Flight

Adrenaline pumping through your body is natural. The reasons for the release of this chemical can be, danger, fear, sometimes just good old fashioned stress or for no fucking reason at all. This is the Fight or Flight response. Now, you've all heard of the Fight or Flight, your body gets ready to either fight, or run. But, there are actually four parts to Fight or Flight; Fight, Flight, Freeze, and Flop. Here they all are broken down for you:

Fight: Senses heightened, hair trigger anger/violence, hyper vigilance, stubbornness, body reacts with sweating, and your heart beats faster.

Flight: Can feel like panic or anxiety, have to move, can't sit still. Feel like you are always being confronted or threatened.

Freeze: Cannot function, mentally or physically, self isolation, quitting easily, and not wanting to interact in general.

Flop: Dropping like a rock, can lose conciseness, disassociations, loss of bowel and bladder functions, losing time and identity.

I personally get two of the above. I personally get Fight and Flop. Fight, self-explanatory, but Flop. That's a crazy one. I get disassociations; they start with a strange feeling of déjà vu. Then if I don't catch it fast enough with a ghost pepper (learn about peppers in the chapter on coping) or a super distraction I go into an episode. I do not ever remember what happens during these "episodes", I lose time and sometimes end up in strange places. Luckily my wife is around for 90% of them and she has gotten pretty good at seeing them start to come on. She says my pupils pin point, I get a stern look on my face and absolutely do not like being touched. She also says I usually try and find a place to hide, or start looking for threats. These can last anywhere from 30 min to hours. I have yet to find all the triggers for these, hell, once I was eating spaghetti!

You will never know which of these responses you body will take to. All of them can be scary and disorientating for you and your friends/loved ones. Gaining the control over what your mind reacts to is the key to taking control of it all.

Now you have three parts to "Self-Rescue". You should be feeling pretty good. If one part fails, go back and fix it. You need all three for it to work, trust me I know, I've been dealing with my shit for 20 years. Once all three are working together then you will have the power to work on other parts of your life. Relationships, substance abuse, financial matters, all the parts that make life grand. You know you're gonna die, why not make the time you have worth it? You do not want to be remembered as a sullen mess, it is time to take your life back and be remembered as someone who overcame what many cannot. So Fuck-it and move on. Now let's fine tune some of the stages.

"We are all alone, born alone, die alone, and—in spite of True Romance magazines—we shall all someday look back on our lives and see that, in spite of our company, we were alone the whole way. I do not say lonely—at least, not all the time—but essentially, and finally alone. This is what makes your self-respect so important, and I don't see how you can respect yourself if you must look in the hearts and minds of others for your happiness."

– Hunter S. Thompson

Chapter 1 Questions and Notes

What are your fears?

____

____

____

What are your known triggers?

____

____

____

How do you handle triggers?

____

____

____

What type of fight or flight do you get?

____

____

____

NOTES

2: Mind over body/Body over mind

This section sounds complicated, but it really isn't complicated at all. Mind over body/Body over mind, is the practice of using your mind and body to take control over each other. Putting you in control of how you feel and react. Not everyone can simply say fuck-it and that's that, it may take some tricks to get there.

The simplest way to achieve this is to get to know your body again, every creak, thump, pain, and mole. I didn't look at myself in the mirror for eight years, so this part was an eye opener for me.

This all starts by finding a quiet place and lying down, it can be your bedroom, a basement, even your backyard if need be. Make sure you are in a comfortable position, lie flat, and close your eyes. No music allowed during this part, zero back ground noise would be ideal, but as quiet as you can realistically get it.

Now, listen to your body. Feel yourself breathe. Listen to your heart beat as it pumps blood through your body, you may hear an occasional skip, and that's ok. (this happens to everyone no matter who you are, the first few times you feel it you will feel a rush of adrenaline cause it's fucking scary, but completely harmless.) Listen to your lungs, feel the air going in and out. Take normal breaths; don't try deep breathing quite yet. Examine the insides of your eye lids; flex every muscle starting with your toes. Feel the sore ones. Flex them one by one and then relax them, start at the toes and work up to your scalp. This should not be rushed; you need to take all the time you need. If you are like me you've ignored pain and strange feelings in your body, you now need a reintroduction. While you are doing this you need to know and feel that you are alive, your heart is beating, your blood is pumping, and pain is your friend.

Take note of areas of your body that cause you stress. Areas that give you a rush of fear or anxiety, these are the areas that you should go over several times in your future lay down sessions.

Once you've completed getting to know your body again on the inside, (You'll do this every chance you get until you are comfortable with how you feel) now it's time to see yourself again, really see yourself. So strip down to your birthday suit, and take a good look at yourself in the mirror, really look at yourself. All the flaws and the aging that has happened since you were young. This is YOU. Accept who YOU are. All the flaws, the gut covering your once pronounced 6-pack, the scars and all. Feel them with your hands, scars especially.

Then it is time to do what a lot of us haven't done in years, look yourself straight in the eyes. Try to look into your soul, feel the moment. Examine the color of your eyes; look for specks of color you may have never noticed. Then just stare, telling yourself it's time for a change, this is to let yourself know that you are now back in control of your meat bag. That you and only YOU can control what you feel. You are, and until you die are going to be in charge of what and how you feel from now on.

These exercises need to be done until you don't flinch or feel anything while you do them. They do not have to be done every day, or in any order. One day you can do the mirror and the next day the lie down. It's up to you, cause guess why? YOU are in control now. You control your mind, and your body. You control how you feel. Taking control of these is a big step in a lot of our lives, we've given in to the illnesses, and we've let them dictate how our days go. Take it all back and be a bad-ass professional ass-kicker again.

When I started doing this I was so detached from my body I didn't even recognize it. Scars I didn't remember getting, noticing my chest hair is turning gray, it was just like I was looking at someone else. It is a real eye opener that is for sure. Over time you start to remember the scars, the meaning of the tattoos you've gotten. You start to recognize yourself. The old saying, "I know it like the back of my hand." This saying does not usually apply to people suffering with PTSD.

"If you are distressed by anything external, the pain is not due to the thing itself, but to your estimate of it; and this you have the power to revoke at any moment."
— Marcus Aurelius

Chapter 2 Questions and Notes

What did you find that was new in your body?

____

____

____

____

What new did you find on your body?

____

____

____

How do you feel about yourself physically?

____

____

____

____

Are you going to keep up the exercises?

____

____

NOTES

3: Coping

During your transition period into "Self-Rescue" there will be times you have anxiety and/or panic attacks. So here are some coping strategies for those times. Some are the "usual shit" spouted by those with a PhD, and others that actually work. So I'll list everything I'm aware of, and you use what works for you. If you have one not listed here that currently works for you, then by all means continue to use it.

The Usual Shit

Here is the usual shit you hear. Starting with the most used by the VA and its cronies:

Breathe. This one is a given. If you were in full panic mode, ready to go fight a tree and eat rocks, they would tell you to just "breathe". This is a "No shit? I was just gonna hold my fuckin' breath." It may work for some, if you've forgotten to breathe, or find deep breathing relaxing. But some situations you cannot do this, I get disassociations, so I am not aware of what I am doing, no one would dare try and tell me to breathe, and they most likely would get smacked in the mouth. Some say it centers you, relaxes you and a nerve in your chest that controls anxiety, but it's not a first go to when your brain has turned against you. By the time you try and start breathing exercises, it may be too late and you're headed for full panic mode.

I tried the breathing exercises once, once... I was driving from Utah to Idaho, a 3 hour drive when anxiety started to kick in, soon it was headed for a panic attack. So I started to try breathing exercises, well needless to say my panic attack made me think I had forgotten how to breathe at all! So here I was feeling like I COULDN'T breathe, while trying to breathe. I don't know if any of you have had this happen, it's sure a good time. I felt like I was gonna black out and had to pull over to get myself together. This happened off and on the entire trip. I must have pulled over 15 times, making a 3 hour trip into a 6 hour trip. Yeah, just breathe they say.

5-4-3-2-1. this method is not too bad. It's just hard to implement when you're not sitting at home or in a controlled environment.

You find 5 things you can see, 4 things you can hear, 3 things you can touch/feel, 2 things you can smell, and 1 thing you can taste. This works if you have everything staged and ready to go, and a plan. Your mind isn't always focusing during those times. But, it's supposed to take your mind off whatever is going on, distracting you from how your body/mind is feeling at that moment. So as I said, it's not bad, just not useful in all situations.

Now when I used to try the 5-4-3-2-1 method I found a few things that worked much faster, and were still along the lines of distracting you from what is going on.

Pain distraction.

I found this little gem while I was trying to do 5-4-3-2-1, for something I could feel I used a strong rubber band on my wrist, I was able to skip the last two steps. So I tried just step 1, something you can taste. I used a ghost pepper, just a small bite. It worked like a charm! My mouth was on fire! I couldn't even think or try to think about anything else. It was the jackpot for me. Some of you can try jalapenos, or just hot sauce, just a small amount to see how well it works. I now grow my own ghost peppers so I can always have one on hand if I start to lose it. But you have to make sure that it's uncomfortably hot, not a dash of Tabasco, something to really bring you back to the here and now. The pepper has got to have a high scoville level, Scoville Heat Units (SHU) is the official rating system for hot peppers, for instance a green pepper, or a bell pepper has an SHU of zero. Here is a list of common peppers and their respective scoville levels:

1. 2.2 million SHU: Carolina Reaper pepper

2. 1.3 million SHU: Naga Viper pepper

3. 1 million SHU: Ghost pepper

4. 500,000 SHU: Red Savina pepper

5. 100,000–350,000 SHU: Habanero pepper; Scotch bonnet pepper

6. 30,000 – 50,000: Cayenne Pepper

7. 6,000–23,000 SHU: Serrano pepper

8. 5,000–10,000 SHU: Chipotle pepper

9. 2,500–5,000 SHU: Jalapeño pepper

10. 0 SHU: Bell pepper

As you can see there are a few hotter than the ghost pepper, but I'm trying to bring myself back to the present and distract my mind, not melt my face off.

Exercise

Exercise is a great stress reducer due to the endorphins released by the body. You can add this to your daily routine as well, and I recommend that you do. This is more of a preventative measure for most; keep the good chems up in your system, and helping you get healthy again. Start a PT regimen daily to also help with getting back to who you were, if you are physically able.

Setting a workout routine is simple to write down, but much, much harder to actually implement. Start slow, don't expect to jump right into a set routine and stick to it every day. I've written the small workout I'm starting to use. Customize it to your physical limitations if you have any, or for your preference in exercises. Try and do this every other day, taking Sunday off to heal. Then up the repetitions every three weeks, or sooner if your young and not an old bastard like me. Then start doing them at least 5 days a week.

Push-ups- 4 sets of 10

Sit-ups/crunches- 4 sets of 20

Standing knee lifts- 4 sets of 15

Walking- 15 minutes

Simple, but this will start to get the feel goods pumping into your system again. If it hurts, embrace the suck and finish the reps, if you're bleeding or tear something, then you can stop. Take control of your body, you can do a hell of a lot more than you think you can.

While we are on the exercise subject, one more exercise that can help in all the areas needed, sex. Sex is so good for you mentally and physically. Releases chemicals, gives you a workout, and can help with closeness with your partner. If you are healthy enough for it, do it as much as you can, but remember, no means no, and get consent. You don't want to end up in prison for a two minute workout.

Writing

One great outlet for coping and even countering intrusive thoughts is writing. Write in a journal, or start a novel. Writing fiction is a great way to keep your mind occupied, you are always thinking of your story, writing notes, and then set goals on what to write per day and even set a finish date.

If you are just journaling, write what you think, how you are feeling, even what you think of other people, get it all out! Write like no one will ever read it.

Music

Music is and can be a lifesaver for some people. Music may bring up old memories and triggers, so choose your playlist wisely. But playing and listening to music can help calm your mind and help you concentrate on other things besides your PTSD. Mozart is one that is used in asylums to calm crazy bastards, so it may help with y'all. (If I was texting I would include an "lol").

I've found since I started listening to more music for my well being I hear more of the words, so I've been leaning towards 60's and 70's music since those songs seem to tell stories. Today's music is not as easy to concentrate on it they just say "Baby, baby" 267 times in a song. Of course it's up to you as to what you listen to. Just please no mumble rap... Music like all things is a personal taste, find what works for you and soon you won't be able to live without it. Music is awesome like that, all but mumble rap...

Countering Intrusive thoughts

Intrusive thoughts are thoughts of past traumas, injuries, flashbacks, all the bad times in your life that have gotten you to where you are today.

One way to counter intrusive thoughts is to get a hobby or three. Keep yourself busy with something and you'll find less and less thoughts creeping in. Sitting around watching TV, or moping on the couch will still allow the thoughts to come, I've found that out the hard way, over and over again.

Finding the right hobbies are tough for some people, I just don't have the patience for some hobbies, painting, drawing and such anymore. I prefer ones that actually keep me busy. I reload ammo, build firearms, garden, wood working, fishing, and hunting. At the end of the day I can also look and see that I have accomplished something, made something, or took a trip to somewhere beautiful. That's the type of hobby that nothing can creep in on, I'm too damn busy.

For some of you it may be golf, tennis, tying flies, video games, hell, even needle point. The goal here is to find something you look forward to doing, but keeps your mind occupied.

CBD

CBD, also known as cannabidiol, is an active ingredient in marijuana. It does not contain THC the high causing ingredient in marijuana, so it is completely legal. It is derived from hemp instead of the marijuana flower.

The benefits of CBD are:

- **Anxiety.** Studies and clinical trials are exploring the common report that CBD can reduce anxiety.
- **Insomnia.** Studies suggest that CBD may help with both falling asleep and staying asleep.
- **Chronic pain.** Further human studies are needed to substantiate claims that CBD helps control pain. One animal study from the *European Journal of Pain* suggests CBD could help lower pain and inflammation due to arthritis when applied to skin. Other research identifies how CBD may inhibit inflammatory and neuropathic pain, which are difficult to treat.
- **Addiction**. CBD can help lower cravings for tobacco and heroin under certain conditions, according to some research in humans. Animal models of addiction suggest it may also help lessen cravings for alcohol, cannabis, opiates, and stimulants. (Information used with

permission from Harvard Medical School.)

So you can see the possible benefits of using CBD as a short term coping tool. Personally it doesn't work for me, but neither does medical marijuana. So try CBD, it is available all over, and decide for yourself its benefits.

Suicide

The big S. The last on the list of coping. It is not a coping strategy, in fact it is taking the easy way out, but sometimes people use it to cope. When you feel there is nothing else you can do, no way can you handle life anymore. Trust me, I've been there. Before I found my "Self-Rescue" I even tried to kill myself.

As it's been told; "Suicide is a permanent solution to a temporary problem". It is a permanent solution for a temporary situation; you may feel like all is lost, no hope, no help. The system has failed you, family has failed you. But, remember, YOU can now help yourself; YOU can control your life. Feelings are temporary, stress is temporary, and if you are patient enough, so is life.

If you truly are thinking of hurting yourself, talk to someone, even if it's with yourself. If you really are thinking about it and talking hasn't helped please call the new suicide help line at: 988. Worst case you can be on hold for an hour and you'll get bored and start watching porn. Problem solved.

Many (including me) didn't and don't think about the far reaches of suicide. Of course if you go through with it, you are away from your stress, burning in hell, (maybe, sounds better that way) while your loved ones suffer from your act. All the while the problem you died for is something that would have passed. Pebbles feel like boulders when you are down and out. Follow my steps; you'll hopefully not get into the position of wanting to hurt yourself again.

Finally, in the words every cadre in Ranger school: "Embrace the suck". Own it.

"If you're going through hell,
keep going."
-Winston Churchill

"One day you will tell your story of how you've overcome what you are going through now and it will become part of someone's survival guide."

-Unknown

"If you can't fly, then run. If you can't run, then walk. If you can't walk, then crawl. But whatever you do, you have to keep moving forward"

– Martin Luther King Jr.

Chapter 3 Questions and Notes

How have you coped in the past?

____

____

____

____

What is the hardest symptom to cope with?

____

____

____

____

Are you going to use any of the above strategies?

____

____

Which strategy will you use the most, and the
least?

____

____

____

____

NOTES

4: Being Your Best Self

This chapter is about being your best self, being who you want to be. This means doing everything up to this point in the book, and what follows, and THEN becoming who you want to be and who you deserve to be.

For roughly 17 years I was not who I wanted to be, but I didn't care during that time, I was completely lost. I floated day-to-day, ending up at the bottom of a bottle daily. I floated through being a husband, Father, brother, son and Friend. I was a functional alcoholic so a lot of people I met during that time thought that was the real me, it wasn't even close. I even had a whole marriage during that time, it wasn't me. I didn't care, but pretended I did.

I was good at hiding a lot of things, pretended to function during bad periods. I had excuses for losing jobs, not taking care of myself and such. I would blame it on alcohol, but it wasn't the alcohol at all, in fact if it wasn't for the Vodka I would have been worse! I was crawling into myself and hiding from the world, putting on a smile and a joke to get through all those tough moments. I wasn't able to enjoy my kids, and I wasn't able to grieve when my Father passed away. I was mentally and emotionally blocked off from the world. Not being my best self has caused me a lot of regrets to this day.

This is my experience with NOT being my best self. A cautionary tale of what can happen when you ignore the PTSD symptoms and just self-medicate.

Here are a few tricks to help you become your best self:

Try and think of one positive thing a day; anything at all. A good memory from your child hood, a favorite pet, or just look outside and think of how nature is perfect in its own chaotic way. Positive thoughts can be as simple as realizing you were able to get out of bed that day, or that you have a roof over your head, and food on the table.

Limit social media; people are addicted to their phones; they are addicted to Facebook, Instagram, TicTok, and whatever else comes down the pipe. These apps are teaching instant gratification, and the tech companies are shoving whatever THEY want you to see right into your head. I used to scroll through Facebook and found myself feeling shitty afterwards. Cutting it out helped a ton. My face isn't always buried into my phone and I can concentrate on the real world. Social media can also be a trigger; you never know what you are going to see on there. It's better to just leave it to the younger generations and let them destroy their own minds.

Having something to look forward to; having a plan for an event, a trip, or even expecting a package can give you a positive outlook for the day. Looking forward to a trip to Vegas, or hunting season can give you something to make life bearable. Plans set in the future give you a reason to want to wake up each morning. Even something as simple as waiting for a package to arrive can give you something to look forward to.

Writing yourself sticky notes; this may seem kind of cheesy to some, but it works wonders for mindset. On your good days write yourself a sticky note and stick it by your coffee maker, or on the bathroom mirror. Write how you are feeling, how you feel about yourself, whatever you want, so when you see it the next day, if you're having a bad time, it can remind you of where you have been, and where you can easily get back too.

Don't expect outside help; this is a touchy subject for some. There are thousands of non-profits and companies that tout they help Veterans in need. You've seen the ads, "Buy our

Bracelet to help Veterans", or "part of the proceeds go towards Veterans in need". They use a celebrity to push their story, and the rake in millions of dollars a year. I've been a Veteran in need, not once have I ever received any sort of support or help from any organization I've contacted. Don't get me wrong, there are some that are legit, the "Gary Sinise Foundation" is one. Their only issue is they only help vets with visible wounds, not the invisible ones we suffer from. I'm not saying PTSD is worse than losing your arms and legs, they are just different wounds, one is visible to the world, the other we suffer with in secret.

I've tried contacting some of these Veteran help companies; I've never even gotten a response. Being a 100% disabled service connected Veteran you would think I might just get a courtesy response, but nothing, nada, zilch, zero. Crickets.

So there are a few examples of helping you stay in a positive mindset as you continue your "Self-Rescue" journey. If you have something you do every day that helps, keep it up!

Seeing the world with new eyes

Being your best self will also incorporate seeing the world differently than you did before "Self-Rescue". You will see a lot of things more clearly, for better and for worse.

Seeing your family, friends, and even co-workers differently can be a real eye opener. The big part to remember is that they are the same people you got along with (or didn't) before. Don't make rash decisions, or change things with them right away. They will have to get to know the new you as well. A whole chapter on relationships is coming up.

You will also see old triggers and situations differently, opening up a whole part of your life that has been blocked off for a long, long time. Take advantage of all of this and challenge yourself everyday to try at your old life again. You are in control now.

"You cannot dream yourself into a character; you must hammer and forge yourself one."

-- Henry David Thoreau

Chapter 4 Questions and Notes

What kind of positive thoughts will you use?

What do you want to look forward to?

Are you starting to feel like you are getting control of your life?

NOTES

5: Substance Abuse/Self-Medicating

This is a subject where I am a tried and true expert. I was a raging alcoholic for close to 20 years, with short breaks of sobriety.

I used alcohol to self-medicate. I was a functioning alcoholic, if I didn't want anyone to know I was drinking, they wouldn't know. I had not only those close to me fooled, but myself as well. I had to have it, and being military, had to be on schedule. At 4pm every day I started drinking during the week. While in the Army it was the same, didn't even matter if it was before final formation, or where ever I was drinking. It did evolve for awhile to drinking during all waking hours, but winded down to evenings only a few years after I got out.

I used it to suppress the PTSD symptoms I was experiencing. It would instantly stop a panic attack, stop anxiety, even intrusive thoughts. I was the magic elixir for me.

Yes, I suffered consequences for the drinking; I was busted in rank and stripped of any and all duties. But I didn't care, that just gave me more time to drink. I would even run PT while drunk on Vodka.

I found myself in a great big hole, with no way out. I wasn't exactly looking for help, but deep down knew I needed it. Everyone around me could see what was happening to me, but no one offered to get me assistance with my addiction. So I continued this path for two marriages, five kids, and countless jobs.

My third marriage started with my new wife sending me off to rehab two weeks after our wedding day. She thank goodness saw how deep I was into the hole.

I am not perfect, and do not intend to sit here and preach against alcohol, I still do occasionally enjoy a cold beer, but I have control now, the drink does not control me. I do not use it to stifle memories or feelings either, it's just something I enjoy responsibly.

The biggest thing I realized with drinking was the fact that I couldn't control it after awhile, it was controlling me, period. The drink was telling me when I could or couldn't do something, when I spent time with my kids or spouses. It told me what time I needed to start shutting my brain down.

Now, alcohol was my "drug" of choice. But, I am sure dear readers, that some of your drugs of choice are much different, but no less destructive.

Addiction in any form can destroy your "Self-Rescue" path. The whole point of all of this is getting YOUR control back into your life. Mind numbing substances knee cap the process.

If you self-medicate you need to get help, you need to get it under control. But first you need to realize you cannot do this part alone. Doesn't matter how tough you are, if you're an addict, you need help kicking it. So don't be a little bitch and go get some help!

I fought going into rehab at the VA. I am not sure how the VA systems are where y'all live, but the one where I live is fucking awful. I was correct in my reluctance to go; it was a terrible time, shitty food, on lock down, unable to complete any of my routines. But as horrible as it was it did keep me from drinking for a few years. But then I relapsed in Hawaii, and then back I went, lord help me. The second time wasn't as bad, I wasn't on lock down, and the doctors decided what was wrong with me without talking to me though. But it again worked. Three weeks of hell I think will keep me from becoming a raging alcoholic again.

Regardless of how you achieve it, get help. You need to get that part of your life under control if you plan on succeeding with this book.

"I Understood Myself Only After I Destroyed Myself. And Only In The Process Of Fixing Myself, Did I Know Who I Really Was."

Chapter 5 Questions and Notes

What was your choice for self-medicating?

____

____

____

____

Did self-medicating help or hurt in the long run?
If yes, how?

____

____

____

____

____

Do you plan on continuing to self-medicate?

____

____

____

NOTES

____

____

____

____

6: Relationships

Now that you are changing, mentally and physically, your relationships formed during your fucked up period may start looking a little different. They may not look so much different on the outside, but the dynamics will have surely changed.

As an example my wife found out that I am more of an asshole when I'm my old self. Not an asshole due to not drinking, it's just my personality. Drinking made me more relaxed and fun I guess. Then the PTSD kept me reserved and gun-shy. When I became who I once was before all the shit, turns out I'm kind of a dick.

It's taken some work to get our relationship back on track; I am not the man she married now. I am better in some respects, she doesn't have to worry about me as much, or have to keep reminding me to shower or brush my teeth. She's not so much my care-taker now, she's just my wife, the way it should be.

It's said that when PTSD sufferers heal the divorce rate jumps way up. Your day-to-day life changes dramatically. You go from needing care to taking care of yourself. That's a huge leap. With relationships based on one taking care of the other, since the beginning, it can be a disaster. If the PTSD hit during a relationship, and you just go back to normal, it will most likely be a welcome relief.

The main advice I have for you is this: don't give up on your relationships! If it is worth it, keep at it and it will work itself out. Get some couples counseling if needed to help bridge the gaps. It will be a new experience for both of you so be patient.

Another big thing to remember is your partner or whoever cannot change at will. YOU have to be supportive in the transition. Expecting an overnight change is a good way to just push someone straight out of your life. So relax and let things go at their own pace. If you can help it don't be a dick about things, I learned that from personal experience.

"A relationship is like a house. When a light bulb burns out you do not go and buy a new house, you fix the light bulb."

– Bernajoy Vaal

Chapter 6 Questions and Notes

How were your relationships before this book?

____

____

____

How are your relationships now?

____

____

Where do you need to improve in your relationships?

____

____

____

____

NOTES

7: PTSD/Anxiety/Panic Attack Definitions.

Let us start off by defining what we are suffering from; PTSD/Anxiety/Panic Attacks. Some of you will have one of these if you are reading this, some, like yours truly, will have them all.

PTSD (Post Traumatic Stress Disorder) does not just affect for the Military. If can affect First Responders, Police, victims of violence and of course sexual trauma, it can choose anyone regardless of what you do.

Here is the history of PTSD, this part is a little scientific, but bare with it, it's a lot of good information:

The 1952 edition of the DSM-I (Diagnostic and Statistical Manual of Mental Disorders (DSM) is the handbook used by health care professionals in the United States and much of the world as the authoritative guide to the diagnosis of mental disorders. DSM contains descriptions, symptoms and other criteria for diagnosing mental disorders) includes a diagnosis of "gross stress reaction", which has similarities to the modern definition and understanding of PTSD. Gross stress reaction is defined as a normal personality using established patterns of reaction to deal with overwhelming fear as a response to conditions of great stress. The diagnosis includes language which relates the condition to combat as well as to "civilian catastrophe".

A USAF study carried out in 1979 focused on individuals (civilian and military) who had worked to recover or identify the remains of those who died in Jonestown. The bodies had been dead for several days, and a third of them had been children. The study used the term "dysphoria" to describe PTSD-like symptoms.

Early in 1978, the diagnosis term "post-traumatic stress disorder" was first recommended in a working group finding presented to the Committee of Reactive Disorders. The condition was described in the DSM-III (1980) as posttraumatic stress disorder. In the DSM-IV, the spelling "posttraumatic stress disorder" is used, while in the ICD-10, the spelling is "post-traumatic stress disorder".

The addition of the term to the DSM-III was greatly influenced by the experiences and conditions of U.S. military veterans of the Vietnam War. Owing to its association with the war in Vietnam, PTSD has become synonymous with many historical war-time diagnoses such as railway spine, stress syndrome, nostalgia, soldier's heart, shell shock, battle fatigue, combat stress reaction, or traumatic war neurosis. Some of these terms date back to the 19th century, which is indicative of the universal nature of the condition. In a similar vein, psychiatrist Jonathan Shay has proposed that Lady Percy's soliloquy in the William Shakespeare play *Henry IV, Part 1* (act 2, scene 3, lines 40–62), written around 1597, represents an unusually accurate description of the symptom constellation of PTSD.

The correlations between combat and PTSD are undeniable; according to Stéphane Audoin-Rouzeau and Annette Becker, "One-tenth of mobilized American men were hospitalized for mental disturbances between 1942 and 1945, and, after thirty-five days of uninterrupted combat, 98% of them manifested psychiatric disturbances in varying degrees." In fact, much of the available published research regarding PTSD is based on studies done on veterans of the war in Vietnam. A study based on personal letters from soldiers of the 18th-century Prussian Army concludes that combatants may have had PTSD. Aspects of PTSD in soldiers of ancient Assyria have been identified using written sources from 1300 to 600 BCE. These Assyrian soldiers would undergo a three-year rotation of combat before being allowed to return home, and were reported to have faced immense challenges in reconciling their past actions in war with their civilian lives. Connections between the actions of Viking berserkers and the hyper arousal of post-traumatic stress disorder have also been drawn.

The researchers from the Grady Trauma Project highlight the tendency people have to focus on the combat side of PTSD: "less public awareness has focused on civilian PTSD, which results from trauma exposure that is not combat related... " and "much of the research on civilian PTSD has focused on the sequelae of a single, disastrous event, such as the Oklahoma City bombing, September 11th attacks, and Hurricane Katrina". Disparity in the focus of PTSD research affects the already popular perception of the exclusive interconnectedness of combat and PTSD. This is misleading when it comes to understanding the implications and extent of PTSD as a neurological disorder. Dating back to the definition of Gross stress reaction in the DSM-I, civilian experience of catastrophic or high stress events is included as a cause of PTSD in medical literature. The 2014 National Comorbidity Survey reports that "the traumas most commonly associated with PTSD are combat exposure and witnessing among men and rape and sexual molestation among women."

Because of the initial overt focus on PTSD as a combat related disorder when it was first fleshed out in the years following the war in Vietnam, in 1975 Ann Wolbert Burgess and Lynda Lytle Holmstrom defined rape trauma syndrome (RTS) in order to draw attention to the striking similarities between the experiences of soldiers returning from war and of rape victims. This paved the way for a more comprehensive understanding of causes of PTSD.

After PTSD became an official psychiatric diagnosis with the publication of DSM-III (1980), the number of personal injury lawsuits (tort claims) asserting the plaintiff had PTSD increased rapidly. However, tiers of fact (judges and juries) often regarded the PTSD diagnostic criteria as imprecise, a view shared by legal scholars, trauma specialists, forensic psychologists, and forensic psychiatrists. Professional discussions and debates in academic journals, at conferences, and between thought leaders, led to a more clearly-defined set of diagnostic criteria in DSM-IV, particularly the definition of a "traumatic event".

The DSM-IV classified PTSD under anxiety disorders, but the DSM-5 created a new category called "trauma and stressor-related disorders", in which PTSD is now classified.

Here are the definitions of PTSD and its lovely symptoms, the definitions here are from our good friends at the VA, but by no means does it only pertain to Military personnel. Some of the general population can also suffer from Anxiety/Panic Attacks for reasons not mentioned herein; this book will help you too

PTSD

Who Develops PTSD?

Anyone can develop PTSD at any age. Some factors can increase the chance that someone will have PTSD, many of which are not under that person's control. For example, having a very intense or long-lasting traumatic event or getting injured during the event can make it more likely that a person will develop PTSD. PTSD is also more common after certain types of trauma, like combat and sexual assault.

Personal factors—like previous traumatic exposure, age, and gender—can affect whether or not a person will develop PTSD. What happens after the traumatic event is also important. Stress can make PTSD more likely, while social support can make it less likely.

What Are the Symptoms of PTSD?

PTSD symptoms usually start soon after the traumatic event, but they may not appear until months or years later. They also may come and go over many years. If the symptoms last longer than four weeks, cause you great distress, or interfere with your work or home life, you might have PTSD.

There are 4 types of PTSD symptoms, but they may not be exactly the same for everyone. Each person experiences symptoms in their own way.

1. **Reliving the event (also called re-experiencing symptoms).** Memories of the traumatic event can come back at any time. They can feel very real and scary. For example:

    o You may have nightmares.

    o You may feel like you are going through the event again. This is called a flashback.

    o You may see, hear, or smell something that causes you to relive the event. This is called a trigger. News reports, seeing an accident, or hearing fireworks are examples of triggers.

2. **Avoiding things that remind you of the event.** You may try to avoid situations or people remind you of the

trauma event. You may even avoid talking or thinking about the event. For example:

- o You may avoid crowds, because they feel dangerous.

- o You may avoid driving if you were in a car accident or if your military convoy was bombed.

- o If you were in an earthquake, you may avoid watching movies about earthquakes.

- o You may keep very busy or avoid getting help so you don't have to think or talk about the event.

3. **Having more negative thoughts and feelings than before the event.** The way you think about yourself and others may become more negative because of the trauma. For example:

- o You may feel numb—unable to have positive or loving feelings toward other people—and lost interest in things you used to enjoy.

- o You may forget about parts of the traumatic event or not be able to talk about them.

- o You may think the world is completely dangerous, and no one can be trusted.

- o You may feel guilt or shame about the event, wishing you had done more to keep it from happening.

4. **Feeling on edge or keyed up (also called hyper arousal).** You may be jittery, or always alert and on the lookout for danger. You might suddenly become angry or irritable. For example:

- o You may have a hard time sleeping.

- o You may find it hard to concentrate.

- o You may be startled by a loud noise or surprise.

- o You might act in unhealthy ways, like smoking, abusing drugs or alcohol, or driving aggressively.

Anxiety

It is natural to worry and feel anxious about things — that presentation at work, your growing to-do list, a relationship. Anxiety can help you confront stresses in your life, and for many people the feeling is motivating and doesn't last long. But when persistent worries start affecting your day-to-day activities, your work, your sleep, or your relationships, it may be time to do something about it.

Anxiety problems are common and uncomfortable. Almost one-third of adults will experience some form of distressing anxiety at some point in their lifetime. Symptoms can include:

- Feeling restless, jumpy, or on edge

- Excessive worrying about everyday decisions

- Difficulty concentrating

- A racing heart or cold, clammy hands

- Trembling or twitching

- Having trouble catching your breath

- Feeling dizzy, nauseous, or lightheaded

- Difficulty sleeping

People with generalized anxiety feel as if they're always worrying or anxious about a range of things in their daily lives. They have trouble controlling or stopping these worries — whether they're about work, school, money, relationships, or their health.

People with generalized anxiety sometimes describe themselves as "worry warts" and often are told that they worry too much. They may also experience symptoms of tension, including restlessness, tiring easily, difficulty concentrating, irritability, muscle tension, and sleep difficulties, and inability to relax.

Panic Attacks

People with panic disorder have recurrent, unexpected episodes of intense fear or discomfort called panic attacks. A panic attack is accompanied by symptoms such as heart palpitations, difficulty breathing, a racing or pounding heart, trembling, chest pain, stomach distress, dizziness or lightheadedness, and numbing or tingling. During a panic attack, people often feel afraid that they are out of control or even that their life is at risk.

So there you have it, the long and the short of it. You can see that only one of these can screw you up, but having all three is just horseshit. The part that really sucks with any of these is there is a good chance you will become depressed. Here are some depression facts from our great friends at the VA:

Depression

Do you feel like you're in a rut and you just can't get out?

Everyone feels sad at times, but those feelings typically will pass within a few days. If you can't seem to rally, and it's starting to interfere with your daily life, it could be a sign of depression.

Depressive disorder can affect anyone. It may be marked by feelings of intense sadness or hopelessness, and some find that they lose interest or pleasure in activities that they used to enjoy. People with depression can experience feelings of guilt, unworthiness, or low self-esteem, and they may start avoiding being around people.

All of the above are symptoms of PTSD. It all
sounds like a good time right? Well I've learned
to deal with all the horseshit, and hopefully you
will be able to as well. Depression can manifest
itself due to a thousand reasons. Not being able
to function as you used to will bring on
depression, chronic pain can bring it on. Any of
the symptoms of PTSD can and will drop you in
the pit.

8: The Flip Side

Now for the flip side of things. Let's talk to the Spouses, Partners, Mothers, Fathers, Sisters, and Brothers... anyone who has a loved one that is suffering from PTSD.

First of all THANK YOU from the bottom of my heart. It takes a lot to deal with us sufferers without going nuts yourself. It is not an easy job at all.

As a "Caregiver" for a sufferer of PTSD you will find yourself overwhelmed, depressed, and stressed out of your mind some days. You will feel like that is all you will ever do, deal with someone else's health issues. It will disrupt everything; get togethers, parties, holidays, and even simple shit like shopping at the store.

As our "rocks" our support when times get tough you have to remember one thing: YOU are still important, YOU still need a life, and YOUR mental health is number one. Regardless of how it affects us.

You must remember to take care of yourselves. Remember you need YOU time. You need time to unwind, leave the situation when needed. Find time to relax, take time for god's sake! We will survive if you take a break. You would not be good to anyone if you broke down and couldn't function. I know that sounds selfish of me to say, but really we can see how you are doing as well, we may not say it, or even have the right words to use, but we do.

Helping your PTSD sufferer get through this book and actually use what is written will take a lot off of your plate. My wife is out shopping right now, no worries if I am gonna lose it while she is gone. Imagine being able to focus all your energy on what you want to, instead of having to focus it on us? My wife doesn't know what to do with herself; she has so much more time on her hands now.

Depression is a big problem for caregivers. It is easy to slip down the dark hole when you focus on someone else and forget about yourself. When you think that this is your life, you taking care of someone else. Sometimes it is someone relatively young as well. The future does not look so bright during those times. All that should tell you is if you have to get some help, a therapist, talk therapy is great for caregivers. Someone you can bitch to about your life, let it all out. Doesn't even have to be a therapist, can be your relative or best friend. Just get it out, bitch and gripe about how needy we are, what a pain in the ass we are. Don't worry, our feelings won't get hurt, we know how much of an ass pain we are. At least I do.

Take care of yourselves please. Once again thank you for all you put up with and sticking by us when we need you most.

Synopsis

If you made it this far congratulations! You got through the book the first time. To perfect "Self-Rescue" you'll have to go through it many more times. Carry the book with you wherever you go, so you can find how to deal with crap as it comes up. Take notes in the margins as well, thoughts that pop up while you are reading it.

The biggest takeaways to remember are:

YOU are in control of your own body and mind.

YOU are responsible for how you react to situations.

YOU are the only one you can truly count on to help yourself.

Lastly, life is short, live life to its fullest. If you cannot due to PTSD use all tools available to make it happen. Work on it until you are truly happy with the results.

This was a short blunt plan on how you can live with the symptoms of PTSD. It is not the end-all-be-all of PTSD books, just a really good way to get into the mindset of self-healing and finding yourself again.

Stay the course and use what I have written. My life has done a 180 since I started using all these tricks. I want your life to get better as well, live a fulfilling life not tied down with all the shit that comes with PTSD.

To all of you, good luck with your endeavors in life, I wish you all the best.